THE BALLAD OF FOOTROT FLATS

by Murray Ball

Hodder Moa Beckett

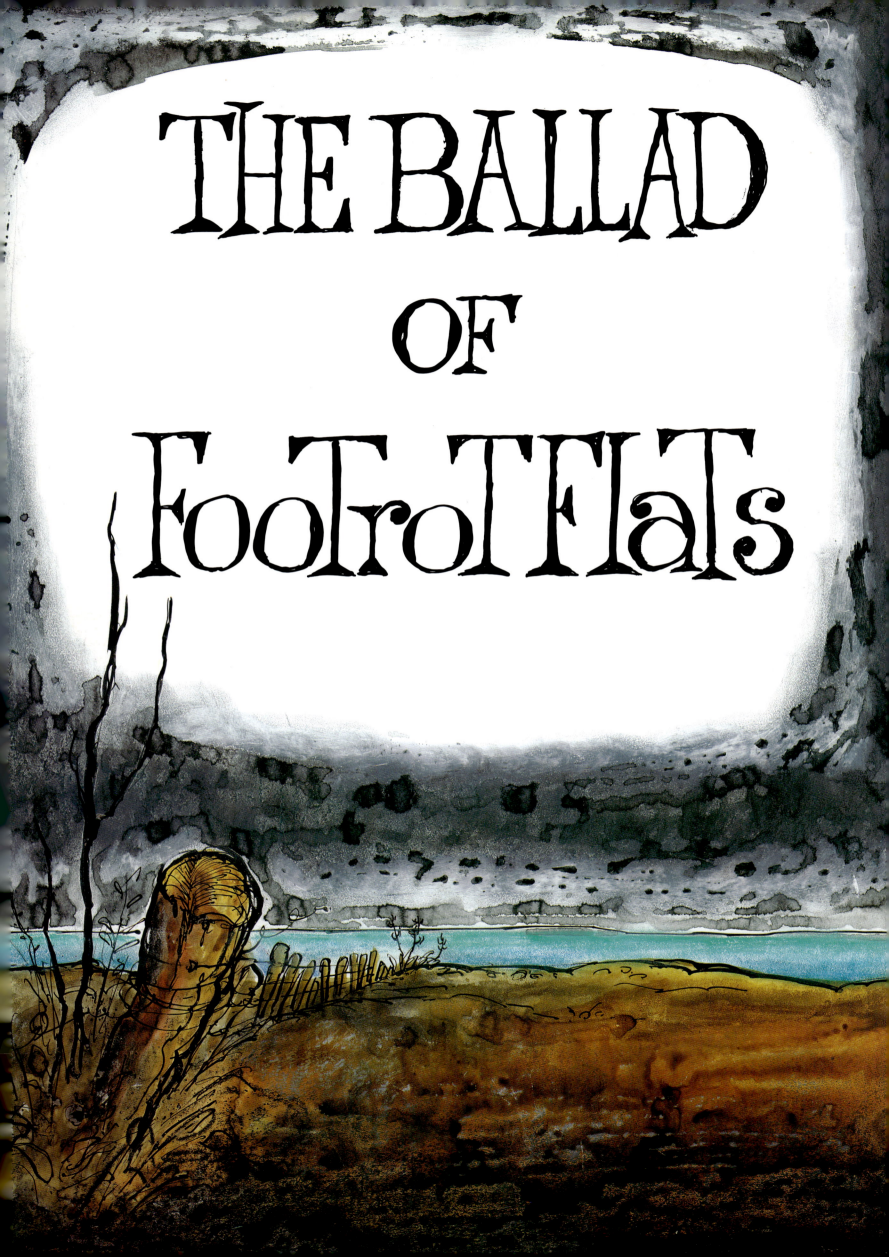

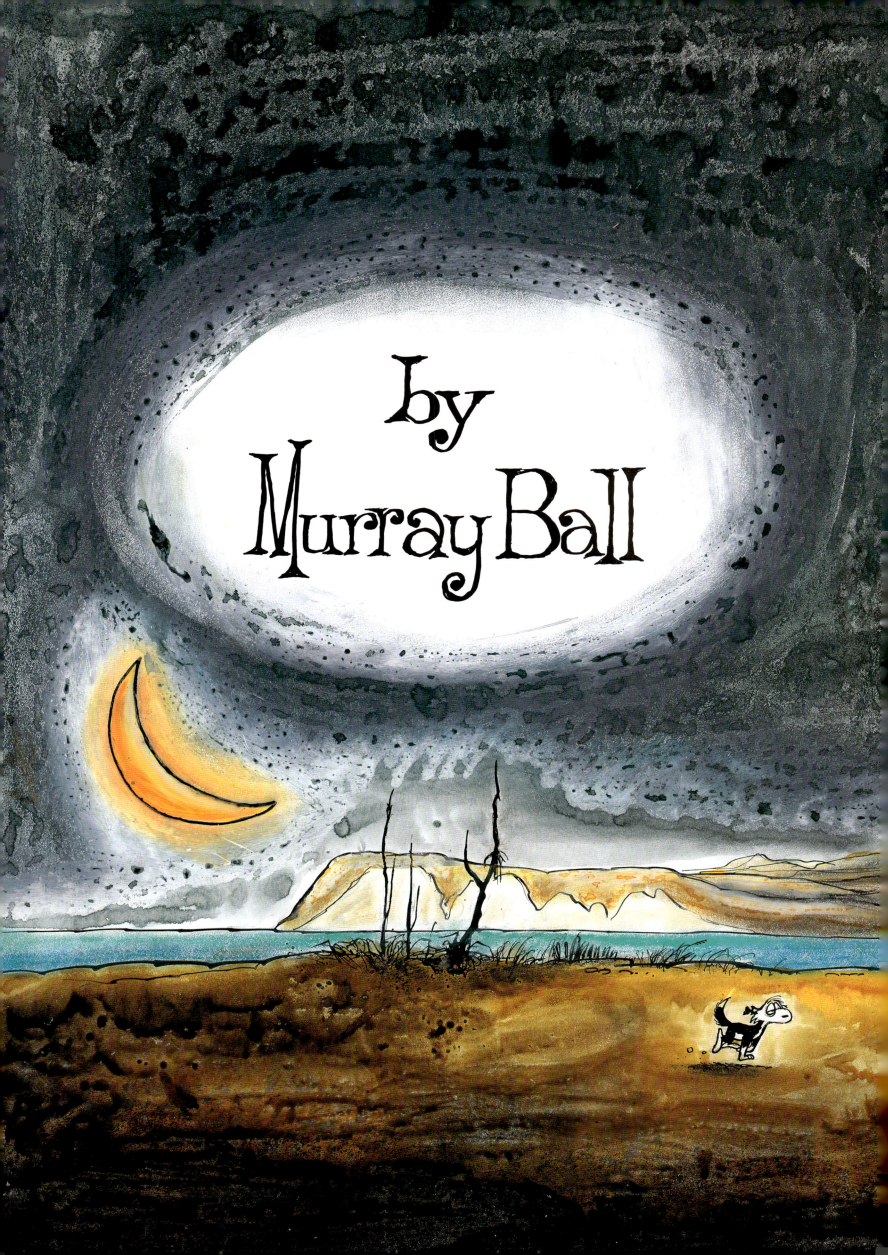

Where the black Raukumara Ranges
Lie out east of everywhere,
The land's been stripped by sun and rain,
Until its bones are bare.

In this land of snarl-lipped razor backs
of possums, deer and rats,
They talk a lot of working dogs
And the man from Footrot Flats.

Some say the talk is legend,
Some say it's drunk men's dreams,
But the tale they tell is of fighting dogs,
Big men on big machines.

It was said they came from Wairoa,
For that's where the hard men stay,
They crossed the Whareratas
And came down to Poverty Bay

They wore tattoos and leather,
Rode bikes like two-wheeled tanks,
The brown and bleary Waipaoa
Threw back reggae from its banks.

The moon was a yellow waka
Upon the sea of night,
They crossed the flats like bleak, black bears
Out looking for a fight.

It was true, they'd come for aggro'
Had Poaka, Slade and Seth
And they'd brought with them a killer . . .

A dog that they called Death.

They'd come to fight the Murphys' dog,
The Murphys' dogs were tough,
They cracked bullocks thighbones in their jaws,
Their bull-terrier was Cream-Puff.

Death he fought for money.
If they hung dogs, he'd be hung,
Death also fought for the taste of flesh
And blood upon his tongue.

He was muscled like a lion,
Full-fanged, fit as a fiddle,
And as he loped past Footrot's house
He stopped to have a . . . sniff around.

Now Death he was a killer dog,
And had won many a wager,
But that's because he'd never struck

Wal' Footrot's dog — called Major.

Death crossed the drain and sniffed the dirt,
Cocked his leg, took one more pace,
He didn't know, that with that step,
He'd entered Major's space.

Major hit him from the side
Like a demolition ball,
Smashed him through the hedge then dragged him back,
Yet made no sound at all.

But Death had cause to make a fuss,
His ribs, his torn right ear,
And jolted from those jagged jaws
Came Death's first yelp of fear.

The gang pulled up, they heard the fight,
They heard the howls of pain
Then Death came flying down the drive
And bolted down the drain.

Major is an iceman,
He is cool, man, cool like ice,
He didn't hang around the scene
To offer dumb advice.

He strolled back to his kennel,

Curled up and went to sleep.

But across the moonlit hills beyond,
A shadow moved the sheep . . .

Wal' Footrot had another dog,
As a sheepdog, not half bad,
And beneath the moon and through the sheep
Came the other dog he had.

The dog had been out visiting
A bitch called Jess, he knew,
Eyes soft as melting toffee,
Scent sweeter than horse poo.

He snuck through the hedge all tuckered out,
Heading for his bed,
The bikies nosing 'round the place
Saw him, "That's him," they said.

"Hard case, eh? He kicked Death's butt!"
"And he's small man, hey? Not big!"
"You wouldn't think he could of taken Death!"

"He'd make us big bucks," mused Pig.

The moon slid in behind a cloud,
The night became pitch black,
They cursed, "We'll never find him now!"
The Pig said, "We'll be back."

Wal's woman, was a classy chick,

Black panty-hose, not socks,
She was soft and smooth as butter,
Rump like a grain-fed ox.

Her name was Darlene Hobson,
'Cheeky', to her mates,
She and Wal' were at the flicks,
Where they went for most their dates.

The Murphys were all at the pub,
Hunk, Irish, Spit — all three.
They ran into Wal' and his classy chick,
Smarmy Spit said, "How d'ya be?"

Spit was a slimy so-and-so,
Smooth as afterbirth,
Came on hard to Cheeky.
Oozing charm for all he's worth.

Wal' soon had had a gutsful
Of Spit's sophisticated charm,
And suggested Spit should shoot on through
Before Wal' broke his arm.

Spit, the cunning beggar,
Knowing Wal' would have a crack,
Kept coming on to Cheeky,
And Wal' fell into his trap.

Spit knew Wal' was no coward,
He'd face man or beast or flood,
But when it came to facing heights
Wal' Footrot was a dud.

"If you're so brave, my fine, fat friend,"
(Spit pretending to be kind)
"Let's do the jump at Mohaka
"And see who's left behind!"

All the colour left Wal's face,
Like oil drained from a sump,
For everybody knew and feared
The Mohaka bungy jump.

Wal' looked into Cheeky's eyes,

And then he looked at Spit . . .

"Piece of cake, I'll see you there,
"We'll see who sucks rear tit!"

God made the land, the sea, the sky,
The birds, the trees, the flax,
But to split the hills at Mohaka,
He hit them with an axe.

The viaduct joins cliff to cliff,
Seagulls hang in space,
Girders, groaning in the wind,
Bestride this dying place.

Spit was there, and Irish,
Hunk watched from the side.
Poaka and his bikie gang
Had come out for the ride.

Cheeky didn't want to look
But forced herself to come,
And Rangi Jones, Wal's mate, the kid,
Just knew Wal' had it won.

Wal' came with the dog. Of course
The dog knew Wal' could fly,
But Wal' up there upon the bridge
Knew he was going to die!

Now Wal' stared down that gaping hole,
The river curled below —

He raised his arms, took a deep breath,

Stepped back and muttered, "No".

The dog could not believe his eyes,

Rangi, too, was stricken,

Cheeky sighed and turned away,

The Murphys all yelled, '"CHICKEN!"

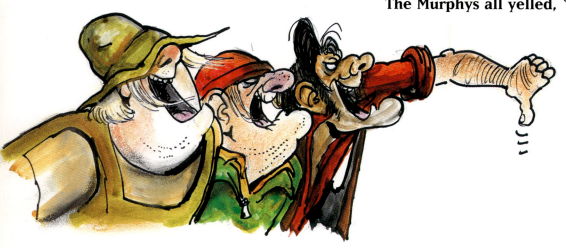

They called him gutless, yellow, scared,
They laughed, they had their say.

Wal' stood there and took it all,

Then turned and walked away.

He sat alone on his back steps,
Remembering their glee,
Felt a touch upon his leg —
The dog's head on his knee.

The dog's loyal eyes were fixed on his,
He would neither break nor bend,
If it was Wal' against the world,
Wal' knew he had one friend.

Farmers seldom stroke their dogs,
They feel no need for that,
But Wal' was sorely tempted now
To give his dog a pat.

His hand was poised above the head
Of his faithful right-hand mate,
When the sound of engines reached his ears
And turned in at his gate.

Poaka, Slade, Seth, Slash and Pete
Rode up to his back door,

"We talk, you listen, Pakeha!"

"Righto," Wal' answered, "Sure".

Poaka did the talking,
His moko blue and scary,
He chewed upon a Crunchie Bar
He'd picked up at the dairy.

He said that Wal's old grandfather,
The crook, the thief, the raper,
Had stolen tracts of Maori land —
And he chucked down his Crunchie paper.

But these were not vindictive men,
Wouldn't take back land or grog,
In payment for Pop Footrot's sins
They'd just take back Wal's dog.

Wal' thought at first they jested,
And laughed, "Ha ha", he said.

Poaka spoke like a glacier grinding,
"Give us strife, Bro, and you're dead."

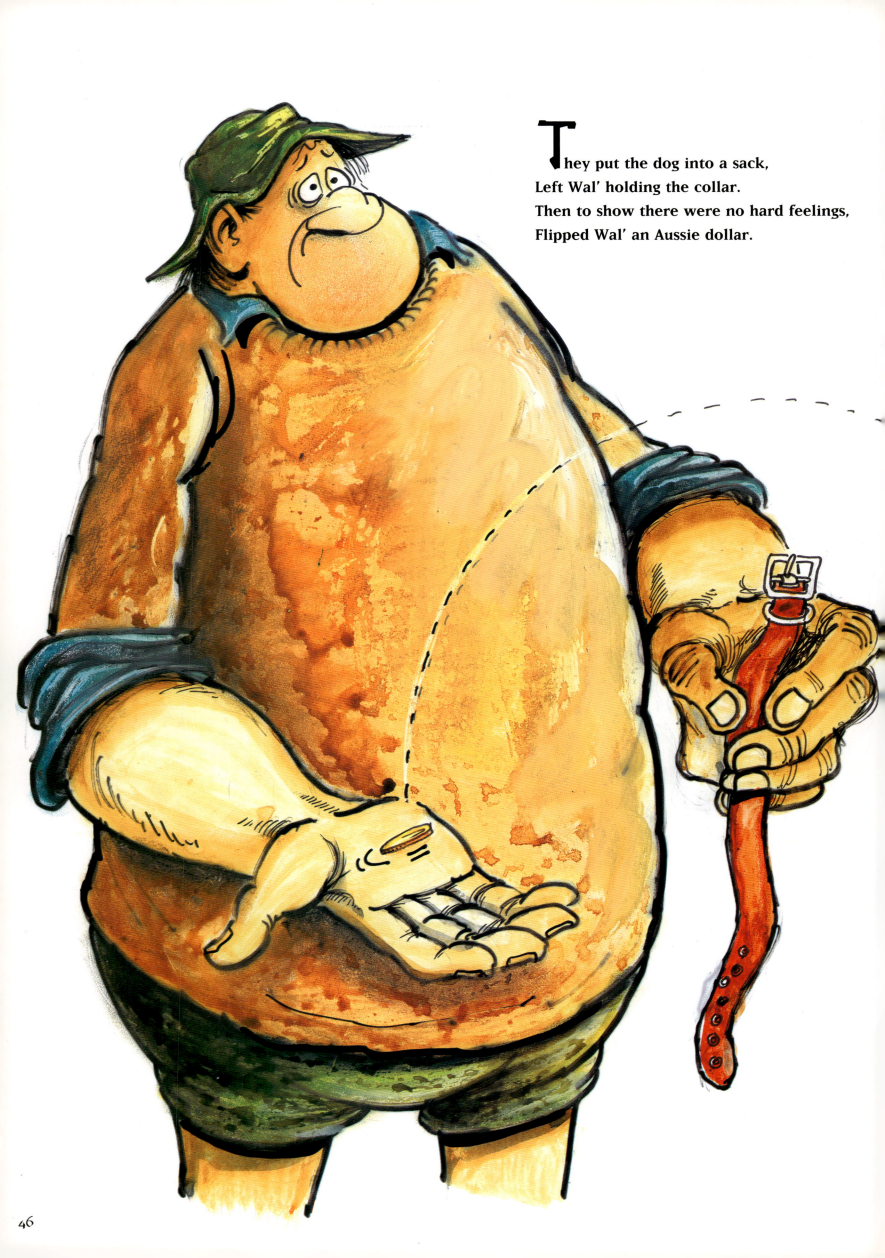

They put the dog into a sack,
Left Wal' holding the collar.
Then to show there were no hard feelings,
Flipped Wal' an Aussie dollar.

He watched them go, white as a lung,
Heard the dog whine, heard them laugh,
The silence screamed, "You're a coward, Wal' "
And he bellowed like a calf.

Poaka had a cat called Fred
Fred was short for Freddy
And strange as it may seem to you
She was the mighty Horse's 'steady'.

I haven't mentioned the Footrot cat —
Picture blackberry, barbed wire, gorse . . .
The Yanks have got the H Bomb,
The East Cape has got Horse.

Relentless as a lava flow
With chainsaw teeth for claws,
His fangs are slivered shards of glass
Out here 'H' stands for Horse.

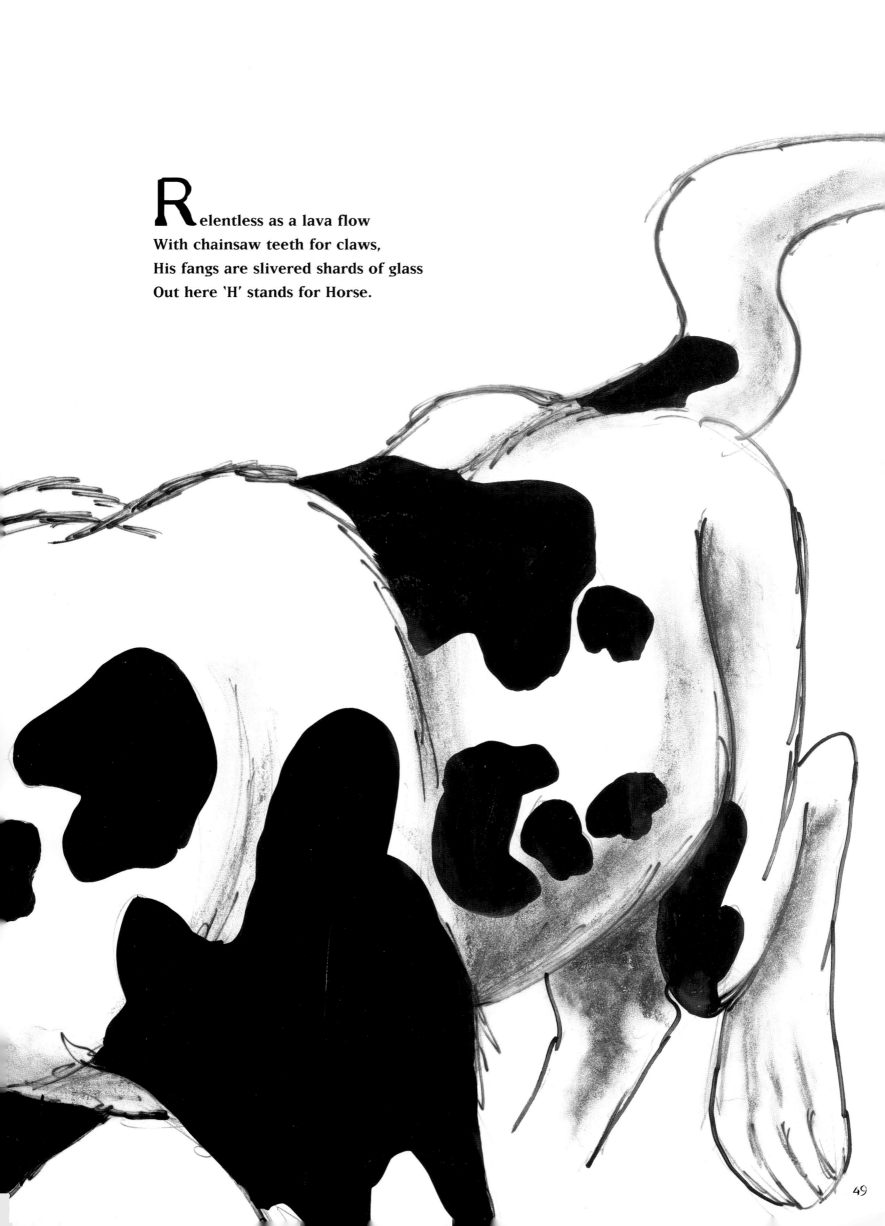

But Horse loved Fred with
a fierce firm love,
And when Fred hit the 'Flats',
Horse followed her like a shark
does blood
And cats do female cats.

So when the Murphys came with their fighting dog
All primed for the attack,
Horse was having fun with Fred,
In the tin shed, out the back.

The old shed stood behind the house
That was the gang's abode,
And in that sack and in that shed,
Was where Wal's dog was stowed.

Cream-Puff, the Murphys' fighting dog,
Hit the floor with all paws going,

Crashed through the door, through to the back,
Hit the tin shed without slowing.

Horse was in the midst of showing
Fred how much he cared
But broke off for a moment
To attend Cream-Puff instead.

Horse hit him with a left, a right
That sliced off lumps of skin,

And Cream-Puff he came flying out
Twice as fast as he'd flown in.

Back down the hall and out the door
Leaving blood squirts up the wall,
Straight into the Murphys' ute
And would not come out at all.

Meanwhile a nose pushed through the sack,
And then the dog, complete.
He scuttled through the shattered door
And hit Poaka's feet.

Poaka smirked, "No contest!"
"Beat your dog, eh? No sweat,"
"We didn't see it," Irish whined,
"No fight, no proof, no bet!"

The Murphys bitched and belly-ached
That the fight had not been fair,
But Poaka, Pete and Slash and them,
Said the dog had won it square.

The Murphys were not happy but payed
The piper for his tune,
But Irish growled as they drove away,
"I'll have that dog — real soon!"

Now Rangi Jones was at the house,
His cousin was Red Pete,
He'd ridden back with his cuz's mates
When he'd seen how Wal'd been beat.

But Rangi *knew* the dog was Wal's
And to get it back,
Wal' would have to get his arse in gear
And seize it from the pack!

Wal' Footrot lay in bed that night
Awake, he could not sleep.
At last he threw the blankets off
And vowed he'd make the leap.

It was a hollow, moaning dawn,
The wind bit like a trap,
Wal' stood high on the bridge that spanned
The deep Mohaka Gap.

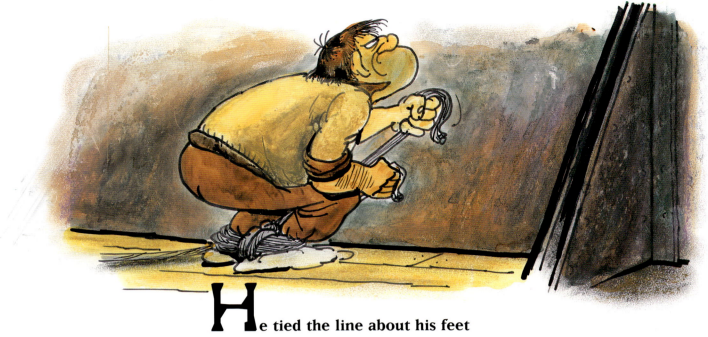

He tied the line about his feet
With hands that shook like leaves,

Moved to the edge, took a deep breath . . .

And sank down to his knees.

H
e was crawling back along the bridge,
More a cockroach than a man,
When Rangi Jones came to his side
And told him the gang's plan.

"They're taking off, they're heading out
To fight the dog!" he said,
"They'll be here soon, on the road down there —
You got to save him — or he's dead!"

Wal' looked down and saw the bikes
And his soft heart missed a beat,
The dog was clutched to the hairy chest
Of Rangi's cuz', Red Pete.

"I'll tie your feet, then you can jump."
Said the boy as the east wind sang.
A tear rolled down Wal's ruddy cheek,

"I just can't do it, Rang'."

63

The bikes were now approaching fast
The wind belched, blew and sucked,
Rangi strapped on the bungy cord

And leapt off the viaduct!

Rangi sailed back with the dog,
So far neither hurt,
As he started to fall again
Wal' grabbed him by his shirt.

For a moment Time stood still,
Their lives hung by a sliver,
Would Wal's grip hold and pull them back,
Or would they all die in the river?

Hanging high above the void
Wal's head began to spin,
He felt himself begin to fall,
Sweat dripped from his chin.

His grip started to loosen,
He'd have to let them go . . .
Then a hand reached over his,
And a voice he knew said, "Whoa."

Wal' was pulled back, Rangi too,
The dog made doggy noise,
Wal' looked past its licking tongue,
Saw Murphy and his boys.

"Decent of you, Irish, Mate,"
Said Wal', "we was in the bog."

"Well now, you just crawl off to your hole,"
Said Spit, "We'll take the dog."

Wal' rose carefully to his feet,
To face the Murphys in a line,
"Get out of it, ya pack of thieves,
You know the dog is mine!"

"Finders keepers! We saved his hide,
He'd be gone if it'd been left to you."
"He's mine", said Wal' and turned to go . . .

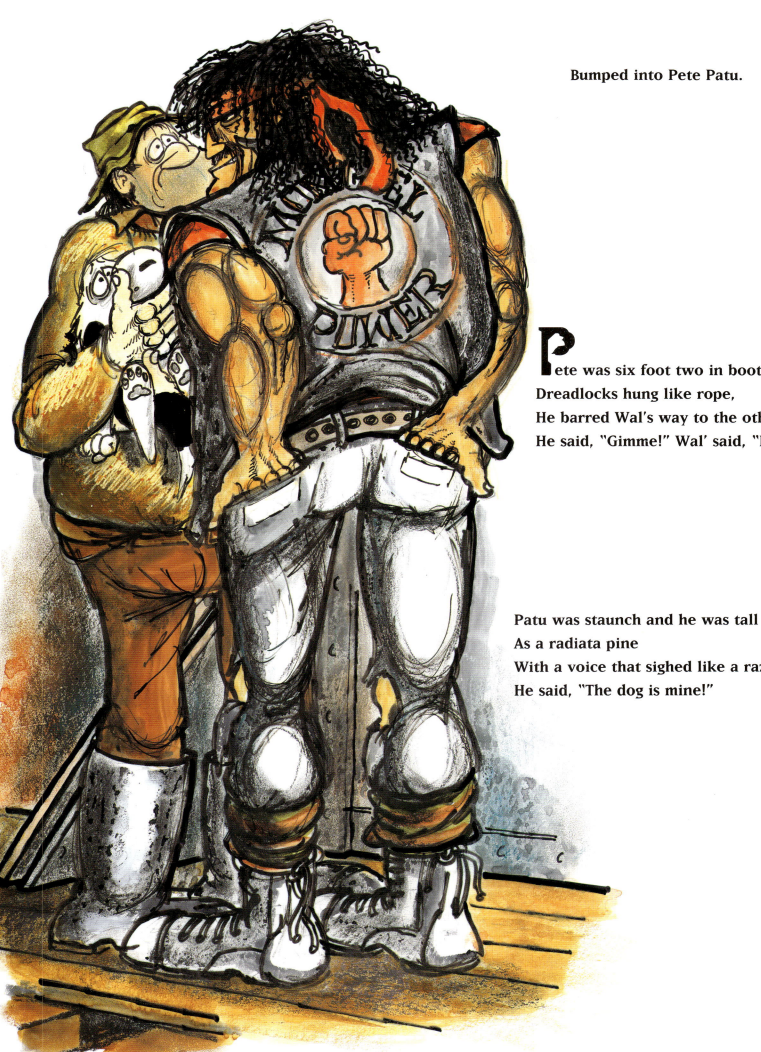

Bumped into Pete Patu.

Pete was six foot two in boots,
Dreadlocks hung like rope,
He barred Wal's way to the other end,
He said, "Gimme!" Wal' said, "Nope."

Patu was staunch and he was tall
As a radiata pine
With a voice that sighed like a razor slit,
He said, "The dog is mine!"

W al' looked Red Pete straight in the neck
A heavy silence fell
Wal' looked down and thought a bit,

Looked up, and said, "Like hell!"

Red Pete didn't rate him,
He knew Wal' couldn't hack it,
So he bellied up to take the dog
And stuff it in his jacket.

Wool-greased knuckles clamped Pete's throat
With a healthy sheep-yard smell
Wal' Footrot's face right close to his
Said soft, "I said, 'Like hell!'"

Before the mob could take revenge,
And Wal' was slashed or chained,
Irish elbowed them aside,
"The dog is mine!" he claimed.

The Murphys had brought pick-handles,
The gang had blades and chains,
On that bridge above the Mohaka,
All they lacked was brains.

The Pig, for all his awesome looks,
Led the mob because he could
Keep his head when the rest lost theirs.
He summed up how things stood.

He strode forward, seized the dog
And shoved it in a sack,
Knotted it tight with baling twine,
Told the rabble to stand back.

He swung it twice about his head,
Above his blue-lined brow
Then hurled it out into the void,
And growled, "Whose is he now?"

Everyone watched in disbelief,
Even Murphy's nose lost colour,
Patu looked down, watched it fall,
Screamed back, "You gone mad, fulla?"

The sack hit the greasy Mohaka,
They saw the impact make
A pus-ring round a blackhead —
A zit on a milk-blue snake.

The river wound on through the gorge
Coiled round its flat, white face,
Wal' kicked off both his gumboots . . .

. . . And dived out into space.

He didn't kick or flail about,
Just dived with arms spread wide,
Not so much like a swallow's flight,
More like he'd been crucified.

He hit midstream, a man possessed,
As if only death could placate him.
The river opened grey-gummed jaws,
Smiled obligingly — and ate him.

Rangi watching, rubbed his eyes,
The fat Mohaka slid
And slithered like an endless snake,
Well pleased with what it did.

But falls don't always kill you,
Or rivers make you dead,
And Wal' took on both with his hardest part,
Which was, of course, his head.

Two hundred metres down stream,
To show Nature is even-handed,
Wal' surfaced like a walrus,
Found the sack, the shore, and landed.

The sun that bastes Hikurangi's flanks
And butters Poverty Bay,
Saw a little miracle
At Mohaka that day

The miracle was not the dive
Or the fact Wal' didn't cough it,
The miracle was, in this land of ours,
An act done not for profit . . .

So when they get to talking,
Out here where the thistles grow,
Of our national heroes
And their great deeds — done for dough

Of our economists and millionaires
Who say the poor must pay,
In our land of empty hospitals,
Where they turn the sick away.

They like to talk of a simple man
Who was paid not a single note,
But dived because he loved his dog
Down white Mohaka's throat.

The End

ISBN 1-86959-348-5

© 1996 Diogenes Designs

Published in 1996 by Hodder Moa Beckett Publishers Limited
[a member of the Hodder Headline Group]
4 Whetu Place, Mairangi Bay, Auckland, New Zealand

Printed through Colorcraft, Hong Kong

All rights reserved. No part of this publication may be reproduced or transmitted in any form
or by any means, electronic or mechanical including photocopy, recording, or any information storage
and retrieval system, without permission in writing from the publisher.